DISCOVERING
ANCIENT CIVILIZATIONS

THE ANCIENT
ROMANS

David West

Gareth Stevens
PUBLISHING

Please visit our website, www.garethstevens.com.
For a free color catalog of all our high-quality books,
call toll free 1-800-542-2595 or fax 1-877-542-2596.

Cataloging-in-Publication Data

Names: West, David.
Title: The ancient Romans / David West.
Description: New York : Gareth Stevens Publishing, 2017. | Series: Discovering ancient civilizations | Includes index.
Identifiers: ISBN 9781482450590 (pbk.) | ISBN 9781482450613 (library bound) | ISBN 9781482450606 (6 pack)
Subjects: LCSH: Rome–Civilization–Juvenile literature. | Rome–Antiquities–Juvenile literature.
Classification: LCC DG78.W47 2017 | DDC 937–dc23

First Edition

Published in 2017 by
Gareth Stevens Publishing
111 East 14th Street, Suite 349
New York, NY 10003

Copyright © 2017 David West Books

Designed by David West Books

Photo credits: p15, M. Disdero; p17 Shakko/Wikipedia

Printed in the United States of America

CPSIA compliance information: Batch #CS16GS: For further information contact Gareth Stevens, New York, New York at 1-800-542-2595.

DISCOVERING ANCIENT CIVILIZATIONS

THE ANCIENT ROMANS

David West

Gareth Stevens
PUBLISHING

CONTENTS

ROMAN RULED AN EMPIRE

For 500 years, from 509 BC until 27 BC, Rome was a **republic**. The government was headed by two **consuls**. The consuls were elected by the citizens. The **senate,** composed of appointed members and **magistrates**, advised them.

A series of civil wars and the assassination of Julius Caesar in 44 BC led to Augustus becoming the first emperor of Rome.

The citizens of Rome were made up of different social classes. At the top were the **patricians**, then the **plebeians**. Below them were freedmen (former slaves given freedom) and slaves who, like women, could not vote.

BRITAIN
London •

GAUL

Marseilles •

SPAIN

• Cordoba

MAURETANIA

Carthag

NUMIDIA

The senate began to lose its powers when Rome became an empire.

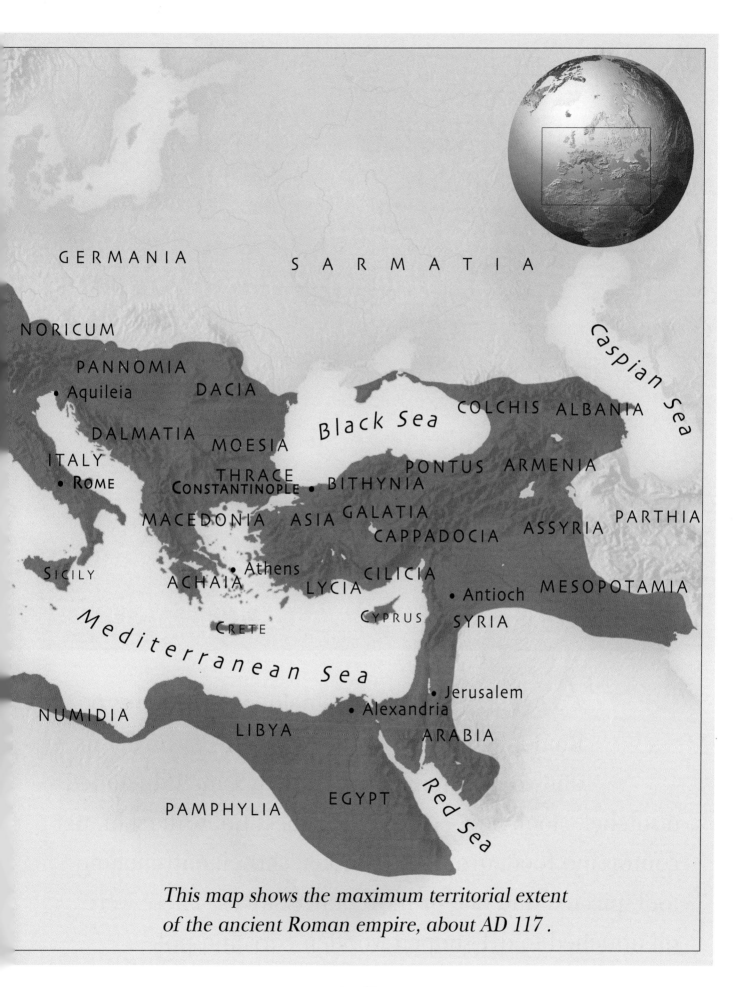

GERMANIA

SARMATIA

NORICUM

PANNOMIA

• Aquileia

DACIA

Caspian Sea

DALMATIA

Black Sea

COLCHIS ALBANIA

ITALY

MOESIA

PONTUS ARMENIA

• Rome

THRACE

Constantinople • BITHYNIA

MACEDONIA ASIA GALATIA

PARTHIA

CAPPADOCIA ASSYRIA

SICILY

ACHAIA

• Athens

LYCIA

CILICIA

MESOPOTAMIA

• Antioch

CYPRUS SYRIA

Crete

Mediterranean Sea

• Jerusalem

NUMIDIA

• Alexandria

LIBYA

ARABIA

Red Sea

PAMPHYLIA

EGYPT

This map shows the maximum territorial extent
of the ancient Roman empire, about AD 117.

A Roman legionary was tough and fit

As well as his armor, shield, and weapons a Roman legionary had to carry his own rations and camp equipment. This equipment included a satchel, cloak bag, cooking pot, mess tin, waterskin, net containing food, grain bag, basket, shovel, entrenching tool, pickax, and one or more fence stakes. These were all attached to a T-shaped wooden carrying pole.

8

A boy waves at marching legionaries who each carry a marching pack called a sarcina, which could weigh up to 90 pounds (41 kg).

At the end of each day, after many hours of marching, the soldiers had to dig latrines and build their camp. It had a protective ditch around it and a mound with fence stakes.

*Roman legionaries were highly trained and could perform complex maneuvers on the battlefield, such as this defensive **testudo**.*

THE ROMANS WERE GREAT ENGINEERS

The Romans were famous for their engineering skills. They used advanced technology to bring fresh water into cities and built roads and bridges that made travel quick and easy throughout the provinces of the empire. Much of the work was done by the army.

Giant wheels were used to power cranes and were also

*Roman legionaries work on building one of the 50,000 miles (80,500 km) of stone-paved roads. In the distance an **aqueduct** straddles the valley.*

used in water mills to power frame saws. Even concrete was perfected. It was used to build the Pantheon's dome, which is still, after 2,000 years, the world's largest unreinforced concrete dome.

The Romans used arch shapes which allowed them to build structures that could bear huge weights, such as the giant sewers under Rome.

11

THE RICH LIVED NEXT TO THE POOR

The city of Rome was the largest of its time, with a population of around one million people. The lower plebeian classes lived in apartments, called insulae, with the poorest living on the top floors. These floors were without heating, running water or lavatories, so the occupants' trash and human waste were sometimes dumped out of the windows. Insulae often

A typical street scene in Rome shows a rich patrician greeting his clients. His house is close to an insulae which he owns and rents to the poor.

burned down and those living on the upper floors were unable to escape.

As there was little town planning patrician families lived in fine homes next door to the insulae of the poor.

The rich kept guard dogs and often advertised this in mosaics on their entrance floors.

THE ROMANS HAD LARGE FAMILIES

The Roman family was ruled by the paterfamilias. This was the oldest male in the family, whether he was the grandfather, father or the oldest brother. The entire family lived together in one house or apartment. This extended family included all unmarried sons and daughters, as well as married sons with their wives and their children.

A Roman family is served refreshments by slaves. The paterfamilias, his wife, and daughter live with their son and his wife, and their two sons.

When a daughter married she went to live with her husband's family.

Roman families included slaves who did many jobs including household chores.

Children brought to Rome from conquered lands were sold into slavery. Some were lucky enough to be adopted by wealthy families and raised as Roman citizens.

15

ONLY WEALTHY CHILDREN WERE EDUCATED

Only the sons and daughters of the rich spent their youth learning grammar, **rhetoric** and **philosophy**. Girls were educated too, but to a lesser degree. Greek slaves were often acquired by wealthy Romans to teach their children. Educators set up classes in public places and even in the streets, but they were only available to those who could pay.

A Greek tutor teaches the children of a wealthy family in the garden of their home.

Life for the poor was very different. Child labor was normal in ancient Rome. A child would be expected to work, from as young as four years old, at jobs such as mining, laundry or textiles.

Formal schools became available to paying students at the height of the Roman Republic.

THE ROMANS LIKED TO EAT LYING DOWN

The main meal of the day was eaten in the evening. The poor, living in apartments, could not cook at home. They ate in the local taverns that served food. The wealthy ate at home. They would often invite guests to lavish meals with entertainment. The diners would lie down on special couches and eat with their hands and spoons.

A dinner party at a patrician's house is held in the triclinium (dining room). Musicians play while the food and wine is served by slaves.

The Romans ate a wide variety of foods that came from all over the empire. Fish and other seafoods were the most common meat. **Dormice** were a delicacy and fruits and vegetables were eaten when in season.

Rome's poor were given free grain or sometimes bread, salt, pork and wine at a reduced cost.

ROMANS ENJOYED HAVING A BATH

Going to the baths was part of everyday life in ancient Rome. The public baths were available to all citizens and affordable even for the poorest Roman. Public baths were a complex of many rooms, pools and exercise areas. After stripping visitors would go into the tepidarium (warm bath) and then the hot bath (the caldarium). Here a slave would rub the body in oil and

In a bathhouse visitors relax in one of the many baths. Baths were an important place to catch up on the local gossip and to meet people.

use a **strigil** to scrape it off along with the sweat and grime. Then the visitor might cool off in the frigidarium (cold bath) or go for a swim in the swimming pool. Massages by a slave or from professional masseuses were also popular.

Bathhouses often had separate bathing facilities for women and men.

21

THE ROMANS WORSHIPPED MANY GODS

The Romans considered themselves to be very religious. It was important to them that they maintained good relationships with the gods. The priestesses of Vesta were highly respected. They had the task of keeping the sacred fire, a symbol of Rome's well-being, from going out.

Many of the Romans' gods were adopted from cultures

Priestesses of Vesta welcome a new inductee at the temple of Vesta in Rome. A Vestal entered the priestesshood at around six to ten years old.

they had conquered. It was not just the Greek gods who became Roman gods. Mithras was an ancient Persian god. He was very popular and became a cult religion in Rome.

Most Romans had a small altar in their house where they prayed to the Lares, guardian gods of the home.

THE ROMANS LIKED GOING TO THE RACES

Circuses were built throughout the Roman empire. Chariot racing was a major part of the religious festivals held in these circuses. The people flocked to them. The largest was Circus Maximus in Rome, which could hold 150,000 spectators.

During a race spectacular crashes occurred which often caused injury and death to horses and charioteers.

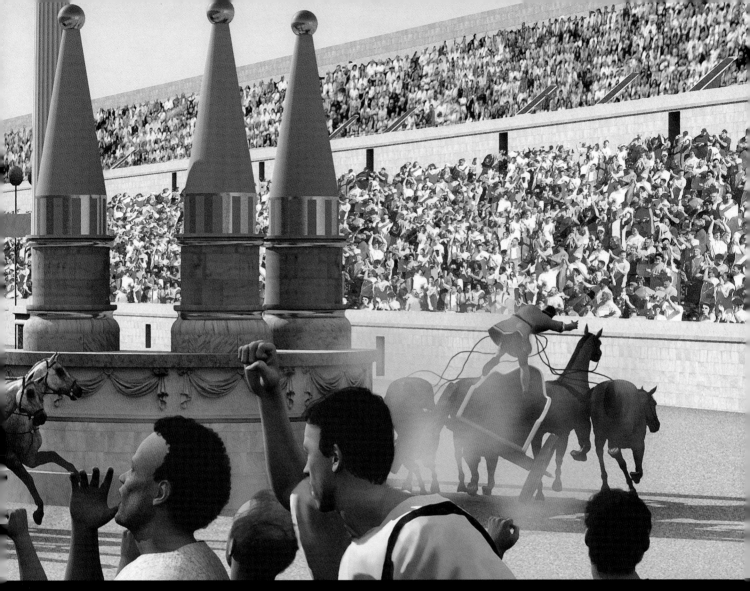

Crowds cheer their chosen chariot during a race in the Circus Maximus. Betting money on the winner was illegal, but commonplace.

The life expectancy of a charioteer was not high since he would tie the reins around his waist. There were four teams colored red, blue, green, and white and there was great rivalry between their supporters.

Theatrical performances were also held at the circus as part of the religious festivals.

25

Gladiators were usually slaves who fought in **amphitheaters** throughout the Roman empire. There were different types of gladiator. Secutors were armed with a short sword, a rectangular shield and a helmet that completely covered the head. They often fought against a retiarius who used a trident and a net to snare his opponent.

The arena was a busy place. A defeated gladiator is carried off while the victor salutes the crowd and the referee signals the start of the next bout.

The combats sometimes ended with the loser being killed. Often they were spared, particularly if they had fought well.

Gladiators called venatores fought wild animals such as lions and tigers.

27

ROME FELL TO THE BARBARIANS

The barbarians, Germanic tribes such as the Goths and Vandals, migrated into Roman territory from AD 376 to AD 800. They took over large areas of the Roman Empire and in AD 410 the **Visigoths** invaded Italy and sacked Rome. In AD 476, Odoacer, a Germanic warrior, became king of Italy. This marked the end of the Western Roman Empire.

Visigoths led by King Alaric plunder the city of Rome on August 24, AD 410. It was the first time in almost 800 years that Rome had fallen.

The capital of the Roman empire had been moved to the eastern city of Constantinople by Constantine I in AD 330. This eastern empire became known later as the Byzantine Empire.

The Eastern Roman Empire endured until 1453, when it eventually fell to the Ottoman Turks.

GLOSSARY

amphitheater
A circular or oval, open-air building used for entertainment, such as gladiatorial games.

aqueduct
A bridge that carries water over a ravine or valley.

consul (Roman)
The highest politicians of the Roman Republic.

dormice
Small edible rodents.

magistrates
Elected officials in ancient Rome that included consuls (elected prime ministers), tribunes (anti-senators, protectors of the plebs), praetors (judges), censors (tax collectors and censors) and aediles (in charge of urban planning, markets, games and funerals).

patricians
The group of ruling class families in ancient Rome. They were the aristocratic families, many of whom could claim their ancestors were the original founders of Rome.

philosophy
The study of the nature of knowledge, reality, and existence.

plebeians
The general body of free Roman citizens who were not patricians. Some rose to high ranks and were known as the noble plebeians.

republic
A country in which power is in the hands of individuals elected by the citizens, which has neither a king nor an emperor.

rhetoric

The art of effective or persuasive speaking. Children of Rome who wanted to go into politics had to study this.

senate

A body of persons who met to discuss and decide on a common action for the good of the country.

strigil

A curved instrument used, especially by ancient Greeks and Romans, to scrape oil, sweat and dirt from a person's skin in a hot-air bath.

testudo

Meaning "tortoise," this Roman army formation was made by a small number of men using their shields to create a moving armored defense.

Visigoths

Nomadic tribes that emerged from the Germanic peoples known as the Goths. They flourished and spread during the late Roman Empire.

INDEX

FOR MORE INFORMATION

BOOKS

James, Simon. *Ancient Rome.* London: Dorling Kindersley, 2011.

Murdocca, Sal. *Ancient Rome and Pompeii.* New York: Random House, 2012.

WEBSITES

History for Kids – Discover Ancient Rome
www.historyforkids.net/ancient-rome.html

National Geographic Kids – Ten Facts About Ancient Rome
www.ngkids.co.uk/history/10-facts-about-the-ancient-Romans